The Star-Spangled Banner

Printed in Mexico

ISBN-13: 978-0-15-352728-9
ISBN-10: 0-15-352728-5

5 6 7 8 9 10   050   11 10 09 08 07

Harcourt

SCHOOL PUBLISHERS

Visit *The Learning Site!* www.harcourtschool.com

The Flag

It was 1814. The United States was at war. British ships were near the shore. They were about to fire on the city of Baltimore.

The people of Baltimore got ready for war. They made a giant American flag. They raised the flag high.

The Poet

Francis Scott Key lived in Baltimore. He sailed on a ship to see what was happening. The British kept Key on a ship nearby.

The British ships began to fire. Their big guns fired all day and night. That night, Key watched from his ship.

When morning came, the American flag was still there!

The Song

Key wrote a poem about what he saw. He called the flag a star-spangled banner. He called our country the land of the free. Key also called it the home of the brave.

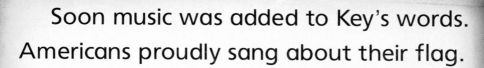

Soon music was added to Key's words. Americans proudly sang about their flag.

"The Star-Spangled Banner" became a special song for the United States. Francis Scott Key became an American hero.

Think and Respond

1. With what country was the United States at war in 1814?

2. Why did Francis Scott Key sail out to a British ship?

3. What did Key call our country in his poem?

4. How do you think Key felt when he saw the flag still flying?

5. Do you think "The Star-Spangled Banner" is a good name for the song? Explain.

 # Activity

Work together with your class to write a poem about the United States.